AMERICA IS THE POEM

Joseph Massey

The Exile Press

Joseph Massey, America Is the Poem

First published in 2025 by The Exile Press

© Joseph Massey 2025

ISBN: 9798315164906

Interior: Dan Rattelle, St Brigid's Guild

Cover Art & Design by Joseph Massey

Contents

The Relief	7
Verging	9
Path of Totality	14
Retreat	15
Here	16
America Is the Poem	17
Pentecost Lunes	19
June Lunes	23
Goodbye	29
Reliquary	30
A Summer Sheaf	31
Field with Houses Under a Sky with Sun Disk, 1888	39
Flowers at Bear Harbor	40
First Sign	41
All Souls	42
After Stonehouse	44
Written After Reading Japanese Death Poems	45
First Snow Lunes	46
Gaudete Sunday	49
Wreath	52
February	58
Embertide	59

The Relief

After a week
spent beneath
swells of
panic,
I give
my mind
permission
to lapse
into lilacs.
June wind
unfurling
the scent—
every sense
caught up
in a rush of
memory
straining
to align with
present time
as I sit
on a bench
by a small
grotto where
Our Lady gazes.
Her lids open
and close
as shadows
wave across
her face.
And memory
stops
squirming.

To be seen
and to see
through
her sight
that sees
the one
who sees all
all at once.
The relief:
to be unbound
by words,
weightless
in prayer,
the heart
broken open,
if only
for the length
of a breath.

Verging

i.

    It's how the mountain
hangs there, in rags of cloud or
haze: ghost shapes shiftless
    in blue winter air verging
on the mania of spring.

ii.

    There are afternoons
when all thought is lost to song
—the vibratory
        pull of God, this ceaseless reach
within any living thing.

iii.

      In an empty church
in the middle of the day,
dark but for stained glass
      flooded with sun, a prayer
held in the breath in my hands.

iv.

    A mild winter, now
the jolt of morning shattered
with birdsong, and this
    dim silver sun, a sliver
lodged behind broken contrails.

v.

      It is a form of
mercy when the rain falls hard
enough to absorb
      the long night's piercing silence
in a rush of wordless sound.

Path of Totality

A cold gust
as birds flew in reverse.
Shadows fell
into momentary dusk.
This is the gift
of any apocalypse—
to return to light,
to the ordinary day.

Retreat

This spring, poetry
slipped from thought.
I kept quiet
as color rose
from winter's muck.
I let the mind
rove hollow,
undone
in sunlight,
unencumbered
by the need to name.

Here

Haze-veiled, leaf-pale
May afternoon
pulses through a window.
How shadows waver like water
on the floor,
and time takes shape
from the pattern of a day.
A room,
a vase of dead flowers,
an open notebook on a cat-scratched chair.

America Is the Poem

> *for Donald Trump's*
> *Second Presidential Inauguration*
> *January 20, 2025*

Rain washes the dust from train windows
as we barrel through the poem of America.
From New York to Chicago, I watch it scroll by—
frame by frame and line by line.

    Rivers and lakes reflect the pale winter sky
and haunt my vision.
    America, what you were,
and will be again—I see you
in silos rising like fists from farmland.
America, the land itself says, "Fight!"

America, I see you in chipped brick walls
stained with faded logos.
    I see you there, waiting
to rise from gone-under towns
and cities spangled in endless dusk.

    We can see you now
emerging from boarded-up corner bars,
baseball fields barbed with weeds,
hollowed-out churches
and factories folded in on themselves
like crushed cans reclaimed by the wild.

  And we see you, and we know you
in ragtag families packed into vehicles
to head to church on a Sunday,
or to visit a grandfather who remembers war
and what it means to survive
for love of the country that survives because of him
and his brothers—gone.

America, for love, we go on.

  America, you defy the narratives
imposed to poison your majesty.
All the poison imposed
to warp us away from our axis:
the true, the beautiful, what binds us
to a shared reality
sealed under the hand of God.

  Americans, may we all wake
to the dawn, this day,
with courage,
for we are the whirlwind
promised by patriots
who fought to the depth
of a last breath
to birth America.
And we are here—
there is no other time—
to watch her rise again.

Pentecost Lunes

i.

without the spirit
the word won't
wash the mouth with fire

ii.

before the word, there's
the sound of
breath being drawn in

iii.

undone, the unseen
animates
a heart pierced silent

iv.

beyond mind the ghost
waits, fluent
in becoming you

June Lunes

i.

blue-green, hazed-over
    horizon—
        unseen geese, closer

ii.

thunder's guttural
      roll; lightning
            spiking the window

iii.

rain ricocheting
      off asphalt—
           falling in reverse

iv.

last light of the day
    evenly
        dividing the room

v.

in poetry's thrall
    the garden
        gate opens, light blooms

vi.

around the daylight
      moon: open
           cloud parenthesis

Goodbye

To live in a place
long enough to know

whole tonal ranges
of color and sound

between shrubbery
and asphalt.

In exile, the gaps
become companions—
how they relieve the senses

swarmed by traffic's
shattered music.
Now, in summer's rut,

I stand in a parking lot
under an overhang
and watch white threads of rain

evaporate the instant
they collapse into the ground.
And the heat makes a sound, eating rain.

Reliquary

No stones mark where the dead have gone to dust
and dust to air
                the soil exhaled
into what was once boundlessly wild.
Fields clipped close,
                      winding green
around a river dotted by silos.
There's a plaque on the side of the road—
dates, a few facts, in faded caps—
                        but the single fact is green
marbled by pools of shade.
                      Of the dead, I imagine
a kernel of bone might remain
cradled within dark, river-fed roots.
I hold the image in mind as summer grass scintillates.
And as the image deteriorates, I give in to time
                        and how time unwinds a body
                        that was never ours.

A Summer Sheaf

i.

    Red as a sanctuary lamp
lit through the night
in an old Catholic church,
        these flowers

(I couldn't tell you
their name) glow
in a narrow alley

        dim with weeds
in the middle of the day.

ii.

On the Feast of Our Lady of the Snows

    Mercy, in this heat
of the summer and the heart—
    Our Lady's snowfall.

iii.

Old windows, thick glass,
render the room mute as storms
gather. I notice
the wind in the way the tree
across the street seems to breathe.

iv.

    Rain plaits pre-dusk sun
splintering
        past deep green branches.

v.

   A room swept empty
by darkness—
       Gregorian chant.

vi.

    The sound of sirens
tangled up
        in the sound of bells.

vii.

    If this is exile—
days given
        over to birdsong.

viii.

   At dusk, how the moss
begins to
       glow in the graveyard.

Field With Houses Under a Sky With Sun Disk, 1888

after Van Gogh

The wind in the drift of the pencil.
Rows of wheat webbed together
by their own blown shadows.
There isn't a line that isn't possessed
by weather. And the hand
quick to seize it—a hand beyond
the hand itself. Even the ladder,
with its snapped rungs, leaning
against a house, vibrates beneath
the sun sutured to a blank paper sky.

Flowers at Bear Harbor

from the journals of Thomas Merton

Besides wild
irises three or four feet high,
calla lilies grow wild among
the ferns on the stream bank.
*

A profusion of roses
and flowering shrubs
I cannot name.
*

Calm ocean, blue
through the trees.
*

Wild foxgloves
by the stream
just where it
sings loudest.
*

Eight crows wheel in the sky.

First Sign

What divides
   shadow from light
      begins to soften. Notice

the shape of the shade
   as the day contracts.
      And how the blue hydrangeas

bunched beside
   a pale brick wall
      sink into the watery glare

of a lucid dream.
   This is the first sign.
      The new season

stealing along
   the periphery.
      And isn't it a prayer,

to notice
   what's noticed?
      The prayer,

the practice, the way
   one walks through
      an unimagined world.

All Souls

Nothing's left
on the maple limbs
spindled
in all directions
like a web
spun over
the horizon.
This is
what remains:
the ritual
of scrawling
in half-dark
morning;
the window
an altar
for my eyes.
To sit still
long enough
to become
vacant,
a vessel
for forms
of weather
to slip through

and leave
behind
an echo,
a pulse.
This is what
remains:
the poem
that proves
I'm alive
in the hollow
of a bright
page. I sit
still and watch
the window
in the room,
how the old glass
gently warps
the one tree
still heavy
with leaves:
yellow rusted
green—a flame
flaring out.

After Stonehouse

October's daydream texture
Quick uncoiling early color
Narrow gutters gather embers
Pain dissolves in noticing
There's nothing other
Than a world the mind revises
And the poem a shadow
Cut through the light of the page

Written After Reading Japanese Death Poems

The full frost moon
is a diadem of glass
balanced on the tip
of a steeple's silhouette.
I kneel in the grass.
Cold November air,
clean night air,
will absolve me of my sin.
Geese, unseen, grow louder.
And I think I'll stay here
until the shattering racket fades.

First Snow Lunes

i.

dusk: the settled snow
turns blue and
floats above itself

ii.

invisibly, they
pass through white
sky—the screaming geese

iii.

with the weight of this
wordlessness
snow accumulates

Gaudete Sunday

for FRS

i.

Inevitable,
the darkness of December,
but notice the sun
as it descends, how it sheds
this sacred, deepening red.

ii.

In the middle of
the night, all that will suffice
is poetry—to
speak clearly into the dark—
a lantern for company.

iii.

In the middle of
the night, an unexpected
snowstorm: soft sparks veil
the streetlamp in the window
by the bed—startle a breath.

Wreath (for the New Year)

i

Burrow beneath each
syllable
the poem unfolds
not for warmth
or consolation
but meaning
cleaved from seamless dark.

ii

Sanctuary lamp
flame flails red—
heart beating silence.

iii.

Early afternoon
and fog in
thick sheets hanging on.

iv.

As if afloat in
the new snow—
an old stone grotto.
Our Lady's
face gazes beyond
the glare, draws
her silence to mind.

v.

Is this the perfect
prayer? Startled by the sight
of a cardinal
in the snow—Lord, your bright world—
words cannot contain my praise.

vi.

The moon's a muted
syllable
lodged between bare trees.

February

In the backyard, bare
trees ensnare the Hunger Moon—
I shift my sight. How
the small blue light makes a point
and bores a hole through the cold.

Embertide

On a walk,
I think about death

until the thought
exhausts itself

back to the breath
cycling through

this body,
a fumbled prayer

vibrating my chest.
On a walk, I notice

how snow banks
contract

into winter's grit
strewn

over asphalt:
paper saturated

into pulp;

plastic crushed

into dim glitter
glinting in gravel.

Marian blue
full-mast sky

beams behind
a neural network

of bare branches.
I stop walking

and look up,
untangling

the knots
in mind,

until dizziness
overcomes me

and I drop
my gaze

to gather
my balance.

Sight fixed
on a point

where the horizon
vanishes

and the unseen
returns my gaze.

Acknowledgements

Thank you to the friends who read and responded to these poems as I worked on them.

Many of the poems first appeared in my newsletter, *Dispatches from the Basement* (www.poetrydispatches.com).

"Flowers at Bear Harbor" was sculpted from language pulled from Thomas Merton's *Woods, Shore, Desert,* in particular the entries composed during his stay at Redwoods Abbey on the coast of Humboldt County, California.

About the Author

Joseph Massey is the author of *Decades: Selected Poems* (The Exile Press, 2024), *The Light of No Other Hour* (The Exile Press, 2023), *Rosary Made of Air* (The Exile Press, 2022), *A New Silence* (Shearsman Books, 2019), *Illocality* (Wave Books, 2015; Hollyridge Press, 2018), *To Keep Time* (Omnidawn, 2014), *At the Point* (Shearsman Books, 2011), and *Areas of Fog* (Shearsman Books, 2009).

His poems have been translated into French, Dutch, Bengali, Finnish, Czech, and Portuguese.

He lives in Upstate New York.

Made in the USA
Coppell, TX
20 April 2025